PRAYERS FOR A CHILD....

by Doreen Joseph & contributors © 2014

Illustrator Janine Harvey © 2014

Printed by Createspace

ISBN-10: 1496033361

ISBN: 978-1496033369

ACKNOWLEDGEMENTS:

I give thanks and praise to our Almighty Father and first love Yahweh, and Saviour Jesus Christ, and Holy Spirit, for this opportunity to help children pray.

I thank young contributors:- my grandsons Matisse and Dillon, and friend Jaynielia, and sister in Christ, Delores, for their submissions; and burgeoning illustrator, Janine Harvey.   Also I thank my daughter Safron for her assistance. May the Lord continue to bless and keep them close to Him.

May many children, young and old, and those young at heart, be encouraged by these prayers, and have many of their own.

COPYRIGHT LICENSES:

'IN MOMENTS LIKE THESE, I SING OUT A SONG', by Graham David; © 1980, C.A. Music/ Music Services (Administered by Song Solutions www.songsolutions.org)

'KUMBYA', old negro spiritual originating from 1920's/'30s, in a Gullah language from the islands of South Carolina, USA. Author unknown, and is in the public domain, so no license.

INTRODUCTION:

I wanted to

- produce a prayer book that is pocket –sized, and affordable for most children;

- That any child in the world could relate to, whether in comfortable suburbia, war torn zones, dire poverty, suffering abuse, bullying, loneliness, or sickness, or who is trying to reach someone who will listen to their inner most prayers;

- That it is an international prayer book – any child regardless of colour, race, culture, creed could find something that speaks their heart-felt thoughts and feelings.

- A book of prayers that children have contributed to, as well as adults.

- And of course children will want to pray for their loved ones, as well as themselves.

- And only 21 prayers, for it is a special number - being how many years it took me to write book 'Perfect Circles vol 1 – an exploration of faith & relationships with YHWH (Yahweh) – our heavenly Father'; and 3 and 7 are sacred numbers for Jews, Christians and Muslims, hence 21.

Dear Lord and Father YHWH (Yahweh) bless all your little ones....

CONTENTS:

1. Lord, teach me..
2. Father YHWH,
3. Bless the Lord,
4. Lord, as I sleep,
5. Dear Jesus,
6. I love You, Lord Jesus
7. The Lord's Prayer
8. A 3 year old's psalm 23
9. Psalm 23
10. Dearest Lord,
11. Father in heaven
12. Dear Lord, thank You
13. Dear Lord, thank You for sleep
14. YHWH
15. I love You, Lord
16. Lord, You provided...
17. 'No weapons...'
18. LORD JESUS, bless me...
19. Father, put good
20. Dear Lord, thanks for
21. Kumbya..., come near me

Prayer 1

Lord,
teach me

How to pray....

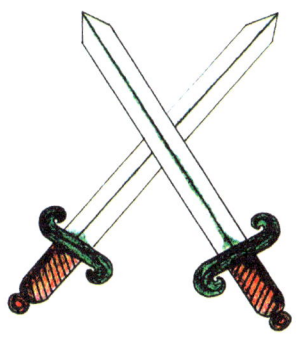 

Prayer 2

Father Yahweh,
Please keep me safe,
Protect and look after me.
Send your angels to shield me.
Send your Holy Spirit to guide me.
Lord, I love You,
Thank You.

Prayer 3

Bless the Lord,
For He is good.
He loves me always,
I am grateful.

Prayer 4

Lord,
As I sleep
Keep me warm and cosy.
Protect me from harm.
Let me feel your warm
Cuddles of tender love.
Selah.

Prayer 5

Dear Jesus,
Thank you for my rest
As I awake,
Keep me near You.
Let me not turn away from You.
Please keep hurtful things far from me.
And help me forgive those who hurt me.
Let me love as You do.
Amen.

help me forgive those who hurt me

Prayer 6

I love You Lord Jesus,
Thank You for loving me
So much, that in giving up Your life,
And taking it up again,
You gave me true life,
Peace and freedom
From evil.
Thank You.

Prayer 7

The Lord's Prayer

Our Father
Who is in Heaven,
Holy is Your Name.

Your kingdom come,
Your Will be done,
On Earth as it is in Heaven.
Give us this day,
Our daily bread,
And forgive us our wrong doings,
As we forgive those who hurt us.

And lead us not into temptation,
But save us from evil.
For Yours is the kingdom,
The power and the glory,
Forever and ever,

Amen.

Prayer 8

3 year old's version of Psalm 23:

The Lord is my Shepherd.
He loves me,
An squeezes me (with tight cuddles)
And saves me.
I will fear no evil.
Jesus loves me Always.
Amen.

Prayer 9

Little shepherd boy (King) David's
Psalm 23

The Lord is my Shepherd;
I shall not want.
He makes me to lie down in green pastures;
He leads me beside the still waters,
He restores my soul;
He leads me in the paths of righteousness
For His name's sake.
Yea, though I walk through the valley
Of the shadow of death,
I will fear no evil;
For You are with me;
Your rod and Your staff
They comfort me.
You prepare a table before me
In the presence of my enemies;
You anoint my head with oil;
My cup runs over.
Surely goodness and mercy
Shall follow me
All the days of my life;
And I will dwell in the house of the Lord,

Forever.

Prayer 10

Dearest Lord,
I am sick,
Please help me get well again,
Guide those who look after me,
To do the best they can
With love and tenderness.
I trust You Lord
To care for me
Thank You Lord.
Amen.

Prayer 11

Father in Heaven,
Please take good care of
All the sick children,
And those who are hurting in other ways.
Let them know someone does love
And care for them,
And their pain will end.
Put Your healing arms around them
In love.
Amen.

Prayer 12

Dear Lord,
Thank You for my Mummy and Daddy,
Thank You for my brother and aunties and uncles,
Thank You for my Nanny and Grandma and Grandad.

(Dillon, aged 4)

Prayer 13

Thank You for my sleep,
Thank You for waking me up today.
Bless all the people who are sick.
Thank You, dear Lord.

(Matisse, aged 9)

Prayer 14

YHWH (Yahweh),
Bless me.....
Thank You, Lord.

(Matisse, aged 9)

Prayer 15

I love You, Lord,
Singing 'I love You, Lord...'
Singing 'I love You, Lord...'
Ohhh! I love You!

(copyright IN MOMENTS LIKE THESE I SING OUT A SONG -
GRAHAM DAVID (c) 1980 C.A. Music/Music Services
Administered by Song Solutions www.songsolution.org)

Prayer 16

Lord,
You provided so much food and water
For all of us in the world.
Please help us to share what we have
with those who need it.
Let us be generous and kind
And share what You have blessed us
with.
Thank You for Your mercies, Lord.
Amen.

Prayer 17

'No weapon formed against me shall prosper....'(Isaiah54v17),
Please Lord,
Protect me.
I praise, and thank You in advance.

Selah.

Prayer 18

LORD JESUS,
Bless me,
Keep me,
Protect me,
And guide me,
Amen.

(Jaynielia, aged 11)

Prayer 19

Father,
Put good thoughts in my head,
And put good words in my mouth,
And love in my heart,
Amen.

(Delores, my friend)

Believe,
1 blessed thought
Can inspire
1000 thoughts......

(Baptism inspiration in August 2011/DJ)

Prayer 20

Dear Lord,
Thanks
For my mummy
And my daddy.

(Dillon, aged 4)

Prayer 21

Kumbya, my Lord,
Come by here....
Come near me, blessed Love,
Dearest Lord,
Hear my prayers...
Amen.

(Kumbya, in public domain)

Made in the USA
Charleston, SC
27 November 2015